# Under the Milky Way

FRANÉ LESSAC

CANDLEWICK PRESS

# In Salem, Massachusetts

Listening to spooky stories about things that go bump in the night—under the Milky Way.

In Salem, locals and visitors celebrate Halloween with ghost tours, haunted houses, and parades during all of October.

Halloween evolved from a Celtic festival. Just as we now carve pumpkins, the Celts carved scary faces into turnips and potatoes and lit candles inside them to frighten away evil spirits.

Salem might be the best place to celebrate Halloween. Its nickname is the Witch City. A flying witch appears in the police department's logo, and even the high school's mascot is a witch!

# In Maple Grove, Minnesota

Skaters weave in and out, gliding across the ice —
under the Milky Way.

The Central Park Ice Skating Loop
is more than 800 feet/240 meters long.
Following the trail's twists and bends
feels like skating on a river.

A snowflake begins as
a tiny dust grain floating in a
cloud. Water vapor in the air
condenses on the dust grain.
When the droplet freezes,
it becomes a crystal —
a snowflake!

Every winter, around one septillion snowflakes fall in the United States. That's a number with a lot of zeroes: 1,000,000,000,000,000,000,000,000!

# In San Francisco, California

Firecrackers pop and crackle as the dragon
dances to the drummers' beat—
under the Milky Way.

San Francisco's Chinese
New Year celebration
is one of the largest
in the world.

San Francisco's Golden Dragon is 288 feet/88 meters long
with a six-foot-/two-meter-long head. It takes more than
one hundred people to carry it through the streets.

Almond cookies, sweet rice balls, and dumplings are popular Chinese New Year treats.

# On Mauna Kea, Hawaii

The sky is pierced with shiny pearls
and glittering diamonds — stars! —
under the Milky Way.

Mauna Kea is a dormant volcano on the island of Hawaii
and is the highest point in the state. It's the site of some of
the world's largest and most powerful telescopes — thirteen
in total, operated by astronomers from eleven countries.

Mauna Kea is one of the only places in the world where you can drive from sea level up to almost 14,000 feet/about 4,200 meters in only two hours. Once on top, there is 40 percent less oxygen, and people have been known to get altitude sickness.

Mauna Kea means "white mountain," and is a sacred place. It's also known as Mauna a Wakea, named for the god Wakea, the "Sky Father."

# In Kansas City, Missouri

Batter up. The ball sails right over the stands.
First base, second base, third base. It's a home run—
under the Milky Way!

Many people consider
baseball to be the national
sport of the United States.

Little League baseball originated in 1939 in Williamsport, Pennsylvania. Today, millions of children in more than eighty countries around the world play the game.

Before 1974, only boys were allowed to play Little League. It's now open to boys and girls ages four to sixteen.

# In Toronto, Ontario, Canada

The bustling night market is noisy
and jammed with wondrous treats—
under the Milky Way.

At Toronto's night markets, food
trucks and street-food pop-ups are
a great way to sample tasty treats
from around the world: satay chicken,
tornado potatoes, stinky tofu,
bubblegum cupcakes, and shaved ice.

The CN Tower, at 1,815 feet/553 meters high, is the tallest tower in the Western Hemisphere. At night, it lights up from top to bottom to honor national holidays, mark major city events, and support hundreds of charities.

Stinky Tofu

Cotton Candy

Pizza

Hot Dogs

Popcorn

Satay

In the summer, night markets can be found all over the city. Besides plenty of delicious food to try, there's usually live music and carnival games.

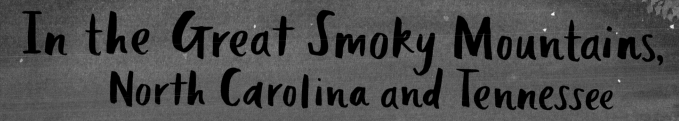

# In the Great Smoky Mountains, North Carolina and Tennessee

Fireflies flash their lights on and off in harmony—
under the Milky Way.

Synchronous fireflies flash light at the same time. The Great Smoky Mountains have the largest population of synchronous fireflies in America.

Thousands of fireflies gather between late May and mid-June in swarms. In the evening, they flash between light and dark as part of their mating ritual.

Fireflies are a type
of beetle and are also
called lightning bugs.

# In Austin, Texas

From under the bridge, hundreds of
thousands of wings emerge in a black cloud.
Flapping, darting, and diving—
under the Milky Way.

Over 1.5 million bats live under
the Congress Avenue Bridge in
Austin. It's the largest urban
bat colony in North America.

In early June, the bridge becomes a maternity colony. The female bats give birth to about 750,000 baby bats, called pups.

The colony's bats are Mexican free-tailed bats, which migrate each spring from Mexico.

# In Washington, D.C.

Fireworks soar over the National Mall—red, white, and blue. It's America's birthday— under the Milky Way.

The Fourth of July fireworks display in Washington, D.C., is one of the biggest and the best in the country. Taking a boat ride on the Potomac River is a fun way to see the spectacular display.

Across the United States, about 285 million pounds/130 million kilograms of fireworks are set off each year on Independence Day.

July is National Hot Dog Month, and Americans eat 155 million hot dogs every Fourth of July. That's nearly one hot dog for every two people living in the United States.

# In Yellowstone National Park, Wyoming, Montana, and Idaho

A billion stars. A billion stories. Smoke curls up to the sky
as we share tales as old as the mountains—
under the Milky Way.

Yellowstone is the world's first
national park. Its land area
extends into three states.

Yellowstone is the most active geothermal area on
the planet, with two-thirds of the world's geysers.
Geysers are underground hot springs; when the
water in them boils, an eruption of steam and
hot water shoots out a vent into the air.

Mountain lions, bison, bears, moose, and wolves are just some of the animals that live in the park.

# In Nome, Alaska

Barking and howling huskies
race across the snow —
under the Milky Way.

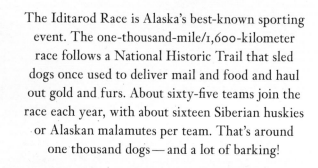

The Iditarod Race is Alaska's best-known sporting event. The one-thousand-mile/1,600-kilometer race follows a National Historic Trail that sled dogs once used to deliver mail and food and haul out gold and furs. About sixty-five teams join the race each year, with about sixteen Siberian huskies or Alaskan malamutes per team. That's around one thousand dogs — and a lot of barking!

The person driving the sled is called a musher. The lead dogs, out front, set the pace. Next are the swing dogs, which steer the team, followed by the team dogs, which maintain speed. The two strong dogs closest to the sled are called the wheel dogs.

The northern lights, or the aurora borealis, can be seen near the North Pole. It is a natural phenomenon caused by electrons from solar winds. When the winds mix with gases in the Earth's atmosphere, a display of dancing lights and colors become visible.

# In Prescott, Arizona

Cowboys ready, rope in hand. Wild bulls in the chute.
Spin and twist. Holding on tight, waiting for the buzzer—
under the Milky Way.

The world's first "cowboy tournament" was held on July 4, 1888, in Prescott, Arizona, making it the oldest professional rodeo in the world.

Rodeo clowns are also called bullfighters. Their main job is to protect the riders when they get bucked off the bull. It's a dangerous job, and they sometimes need to jump into a barrel for protection.

Bareback bronc riding, saddle bronc riding, and bull riding are rodeo sports that involve a rider staying on a bucking horse or bull while the animal tries to throw the rider off. Eight seconds is the minimum time for a "qualified ride."

# On the Indian River Lagoon, Florida

Paddling through star-filled water.
Neon droplets explode in the ripples—
under the Milky Way.

The Indian River Lagoon system is
one of the most biodiverse estuaries in
North America, spanning 156 miles/250
kilometers along Florida's east coast.

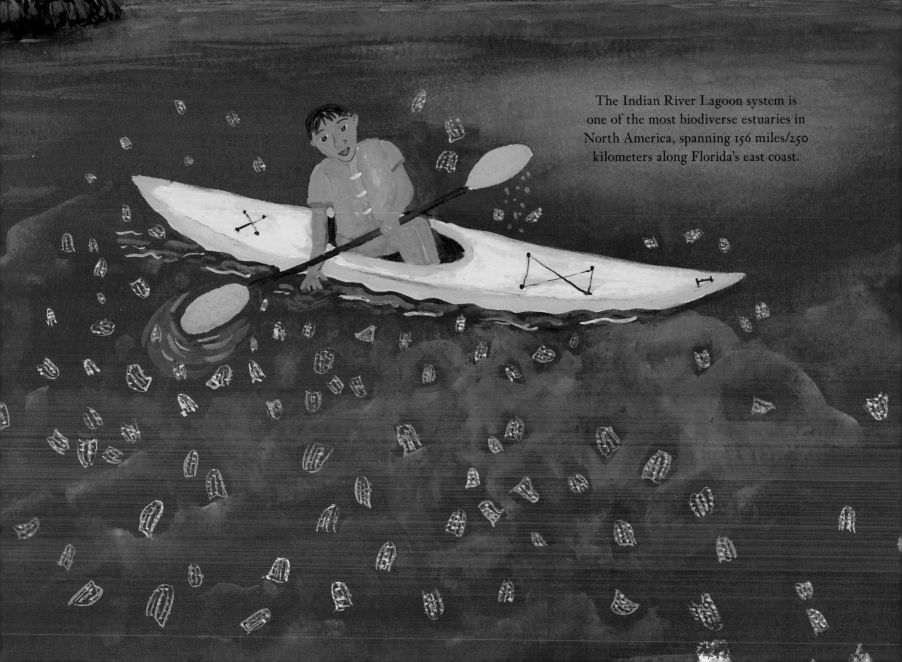

Manatees evolved from the same land
animals as elephants. They like the Indian
River estuary because there's plenty
of seagrass — their favorite food.

The creation of light by living organisms is called
bioluminescence. From June to October, tiny bioluminescent
sea plankton light up the Indian River lagoons. Then, from
October to May, it's the comb jellies' turn to glow. Their combs
act like paddles, propelling the jellies and scattering light.

# In Seattle, Washington

Time to sing. Time to dance.
A time for Nations to come together —
under the Milky Way.

The Seafair Indian Days Powwow is a three-day festival
celebrating Native American and indigenous culture. It includes
traditional singing and dance exhibitions, displays of arts
and crafts, a salmon bake, and famed fry-bread stalls.

The city of Seattle is named after Chief Seattle, famous leader of the Suquamish and Duwamish people.

A powwow is a gathering with ceremonies, feasting, dancing, drumming, catching up with old friends, and making new ones.

When we look up at the night sky, we are looking out into deep space. Our planet is in a galaxy, or group of stars, called THE MILKY WAY. On a clear night, thousands of stars can be seen with the naked eye. In fact, in our galaxy alone, there are 100 to 400 billion stars, give or take a star. Even more mind-boggling is that there are billions of galaxies in the universe!

Galaxies come in all shapes and sizes. The Milky Way is a large *spiral* galaxy, about 100,000 light-years across. (A light-year is the distance light travels in a year, equal to about 5.9 million miles. That's a long way!) Our sun and its planets, including Earth, are located in one of the Milky Way's spiral arms, about 25,000 light-years from the galaxy's center. It takes our solar system 250 million years to rotate around that center.

Scientists have recently discovered that at the center of the Milky Way is a gigantic black hole, which has about four million times the mass of our sun. Scientists now believe that all galaxies contain a black hole, which swallows anything that passes close by due to its powerful gravitational force.

The name Milky Way comes from the Greek word *galaxias*, which means "milky." Against a dark sky, the Milky Way looks like a huge milky cloud, and it is hard to pick out individual stars. This haze is made up of stars and large clouds of cosmic dust. The galaxy is surrounded by a gigantic halo of extremely hot gas, with temperatures ranging between 100,000 and one million kelvins. (One million kelvins is equal to 1.8 million degrees Fahrenheit/one million degrees Celsius.)

The Milky Way is part of a group of more than thirty galaxies called the Local Group. Our closest galactic neighbor, a large spiral galaxy called Andromeda, is home to one trillion stars. That's at least twice as many stars as the Milky Way! Andromeda is so big that it can be seen with the naked eye in the Southern Hemisphere.

The best Milky Way viewing season in the Northern Hemisphere is during the summer months. Using a star map is a great way to find constellations, groups of stars that form a pattern or shape in the sky.

ORION THE HUNTER is one of the best-known constellations. It includes the three stars that form ORION'S BELT, as well as two of the brightest stars in the sky, RIGEL and BETELGEUSE.

SIRIUS, also known as the DOG STAR, is the brightest star in the sky. To find it, draw an imaginary line downward through the three stars of Orion's Belt.

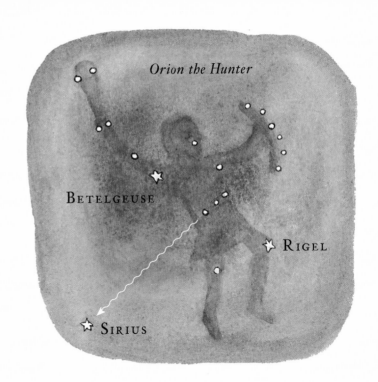

THE BIG DIPPER is in the constellation URSA MAJOR, the GREAT BEAR. It's easily recognized by the four bright stars forming a saucepan and the three stars that form a handle.

POLARIS, also known as the NORTH STAR, is in the constellation URSA MINOR, the LITTLE BEAR, which includes the LITTLE DIPPER. Polaris is the star at the end of the dipper's handle and is always to the north. This can be extremely useful in the event someone is lost!

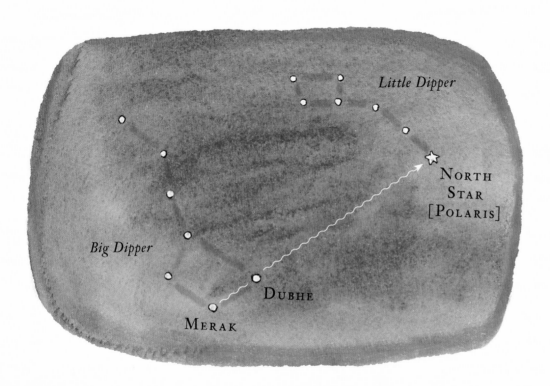

HOW TO FIND THE NORTH STAR

1. Locate the Big Dipper.

2. Draw an imaginary line from Merak to Dubhe, the stars that form the outer edge of the bowl shape. Extend that line out into the sky.

3. That line will point to the North Star.

Find my dog Banjo
on every page —
under the Milky Way.

*For Mark*

First edition 2019

Library of Congress Catalog
Card Number pending
ISBN 978-1-5362-0095-9

19 20 21 22 23 24 CCP 10 9 8 7 6 5 4 3 2 1

Printed in Shenzhen, Guangdong, China

This book was typeset in Archetype.
The illustrations were done in gouache.

Candlewick Press
99 Dover Street
Somerville, Massachusetts 02144

visit us at www.candlewick.com